A guide to evaluating speeches

Chapter 1 - Introduction

Why evaluate speeches?

I believe there are several purposes of evaluating speeches:

* To practice critical thinking skills

I have likened speeches to essays. All speeches and essays have a purpose and it is your responsibility as a speech evaluator to determine the purpose of the speech you are evaluating. Understanding the purpose of the speech will help the speech evaluator identify whether or not the speaker achieved his or her purpose and how effective they were in doing so.

* To practice listening and observational skills

As a speech evaluator, you may have the benefit in talking to the speaker before they deliver their speech or after their speech but your evaluation will depend on your listening skills. A lot of what speakers have to say (and people in general) is non-verbal so not only will you need to listen but also to observe. Given that non-verbal language makes up more of a speech than verbal language, an evaluator is recommended to do more observing than listening.

* To identify skills that the speaker already has

Sometimes the speaker has not given speeches before or has no idea how their speech will impact the audience. A speech evaluation will then help illuminate the strengths that the speaker has and how it may have impacted the audience.

* To identify areas for improvement

I have evaluated over a hundred speeches and every single time I evaluate a speech, I know there is something to improve upon. I keep hearing that no speech is perfect but I think it is the different perspective that everyone can bring to the speech evaluation that makes the speech not 'perfect'. There might not be such a thing as a perfect speech but I do know for a fact that there are some amazing speeches that are being delivered every day that have a tremendous impact on individuals and I think as a speech evaluator looking for areas of improvement, we should not lose sight of the forest from the trees.

* To highlight exemplary speaking skills

This purpose assumes that the speech evaluator is providing an oral evaluation of the speech in front of an audience. If this is the case, a speech evaluation will identify the strengths that the speaker has and consequently help the audience understand a variety of ways to strengthen their own speech.

However, the most important objective of evaluating a speech has to be:

* To help someone else improve their speech

Perhaps the greatest joy I have had as an evaluator is identifying what the speaker has done well. As a side benefit, I also identify where speakers can improve upon for their next speech. A lot of the times when I evaluate speakers, I identify skills that the speaker has that they did not know they had and I identify skills that the speaker lacks or needs improvement on. It sounds obvious but sometimes it takes a different perspective to identify things that you didn't know.

Chapter 2 – Before the speech starts

There are a number of things that I believe a speech evaluator should prepare before they evaluate the speech:

* Determine the purpose of the speech

There are four purposes for any speech: Motivation, Persuasion, Entertainment and Information. There may also be sub-purposes for a speech that would also be good for the speech evaluator to know (for example, a speech might be to entertain but the sub-purpose may be to navigate the online dating world). Understanding the purpose of the speech can help a speech evaluator understand what to look for in the speech. I have listed out some things to think about prior to evaluating a speech:

Motivate
I would look for:
* Ways to identify with the speaker / their story
* Emotional statements
* Anecdotes and stories
* Inspirational quotes
* A call to action

Persuade
I would look for:
* Logical arguments
* Emotional arguments
* The general flow of the speech in terms of arguments
* Logic and leaps in logic
* The conclusion

Entertain

I would look for:
* Humourous stories
* Great punchlines
* Suspenses and climaxes
* Different kinds of humour (e.g., irony, sarcasm, exaggeration)

Inform

I would look for:
* Research including statistics, anecdotes, facts, studies, papers, etc.
* Background and context to support various statements
* Logical arguments

It is also possible that a speech may have one or more purposes and although I cannot explain every single situation (nor have I provided an exhaustive list of what to look for), consider the purpose or purposes of the speech, identify a few things to look for and then keep an open mind on different things that come up during a speech.

* Determine the length of the speech

Although not critically important, it can help give you an idea of how the speech should be progressing and where in the speech you are depending on how much time the speaker has used thus far. For instance, early on, the speaker may be providing some background and context for the speech and near the end, the speaker, if on track, should be wrapping up with their conclusion.

* If possible, understand the outline of the speech

Sometimes the speaker does not provide an overall outline of their speech (some speakers want to maintain a sense of suspense or mystery in their speech) but if the speaker is willing to provide an outline of their speech, it will help the speech evaluator understand how the speech will progress and develop. It will also help the speech evaluator identify things to look for including the structure and how it helps to achieve the purpose of the speech.

* Understand the speech objectives

Does the speaker have specific objectives that they are trying to meet? For example, if they are a Toastmaster, are they working out of a specific manual or project? Understanding the specific objectives can help you understand what the speaker may be trying to achieve with their speech.
Note that this is different from a speech purpose. In Toastmasters, there may be specific objectives to complete (e.g., working on body language, organizing your speech, removing jargon) as part of a speech project while in the real world, there may not be (see the next tip).

* Identify specific areas for improvement for the speaker

I often like to have a chat with the speaker I am evaluating and ask them what specific things they want me to either look for or comment on during the speech evaluation. All speech evaluators have a list of speaking skills that they evaluate all speakers on and I have a list as well which I provide in a later chapter but sometimes the speaker may be looking to improve a specific skill they have (e.g., the structure of their speech or their humour) and therefore, it is always good to ask if you have the chance so that you can help the speaker improve as much as possible.
If speakers shrug their shoulders and say they want you to evaluate everything then you can go about with a normal evaluation.

* Ask for the title of the speech

The title of the speech is the audience's first look into the speech and although a bad title may not necessarily mean a bad speech, a great speech title can help to engage the audience, draw them into the speech and help give the audience a favourable impression of the speaker. It is always easier to come up with a speech title after writing a speech and as a speech evaluator, you may think of a better speech title after hearing the speech in its entirety.

Chapter 3 – During the speech

Strategies to prepare for an evaluation

I have a number of specific strategies and tactics that I use when I am evaluating speakers and need to prepare an oral evaluation after (either publicly or face to face with the speaker):

* Divide the paper into four sections: introduction, body, conclusion and a sidebar on the right

No matter the speech, it will have an introduction, body and conclusion. It may not be nicely delineated for you as the evaluator (and perhaps this is a point for improvement for the speaker) but it helps you understand where in the speech you are as well as what you should be looking for in the speech.

For example, in the introduction, I look for:

* An opener that grabs people's attention (usually a quote, an anecdote, a statistic or a rhetorical question)
* Some background information to provide context to the speech, if appropriate
* The general and specific purpose of the speech

* A thesis statement that helps to outline the structure of the overall speech

In the body, in terms of overall structure, I look for:
* Facts, anecdotes and statistics to support the general and specific purpose of the speech
* Transitions to help me understand the flow of the speech
* References back to the purpose or the title of the speech to help tie things together

Finally, in the conclusion, I look for:

* A repeat of the thesis statement so that I understand what was talked about in the speech body
* Statements that build upon what was shared in the speech body
* A key takeaway (e.g., a closing thought) or action (e.g., a key question) to leave with the audience

The sidebar on the right helps me summarize my evaluation notes and provides me with speaking points for an oral evaluation.

* Write down the title of the speech, the date the speech was given and timing of the speech if that information is available

This information can be helpful to the speaker just in case they need to refer back to it at a future date. The timing can also be important because many speeches have a certain time limit that the speaker needs to meet. Understanding whether the speaker was over or under the time limit can be extremely helpful for the speaker in preparation of future speeches.

* Watch and listen 80% of the time and jot down notes 20% of the time
This can be difficult so practice whenever you have the chance. Remember that whenever you are jotting down notes, you are not paying attention to the speech so you have to pick the times you are writing carefully. Try to jot down concepts and if there are specific examples that you want to point out, make sure to write it quickly but legibly. I would not worry about trying to catch everything because you probably will not catch everything but only catching a few points for improvement can make a successful evaluation.

*** While listening, look around at the audience to gauge their reaction to the speech**

I like to do this for various types of speeches. For humorous and entertaining speeches, I watch to see if the audience is laughing but I also watch to see if the audience is leaning forward, their heads are cocked or if they are nodding along. I'll watch for similar cues for motivational or inspirational speeches. Understanding how the audience is reacting to the speech can tell you a lot about how effective the speech and the speaker are. Likewise, if the audience has a lot of confused looks on their faces or squinting at various visuals that the speaker has provided, this may be something to comment on during the evaluation.

* Write down +'s for positives and -'s for areas for improvement

Putting down simple bullets for your notes can help you organize your thoughts after when you are providing an oral evaluation of the speech (or if not, when you are providing feedback to the speaker). After the speech, I evaluate all the positives and negatives and try to identify trends or patterns that I can point out to the speaker.

* If you talked to the speaker beforehand and they mentioned a few things they want you to look for, write those down and check them off as they do them

This is an easy way to ensure that you paid attention to the speaker during the speech and you looked for the things that they specifically wanted your thoughts on. It also helps you 'offload' some items from your working memory so that you aren't looking for those things AND all the other things that are in this guide.

* Focus on the delivery and not the content of the speech

Do not try to critique the content of the speech; the speech evaluation is not a debate on what is right and what is wrong. Instead, as a speech evaluator, try to focus as much as possible on how the speaker delivered their speech, regardless of whether they talked about something that you do not believe in or is universally controversial. Critiquing the content of the speech may also have a negative effect on the speaker: they may believe that they are right and you are in fact wrong and therefore, your whole evaluation has lost credibility.

Introduction - what to look for

In my opinion, a speech introduction's overall objective is threefold:

1. Introduce the audience to the speech by providing background and context for the speech - Many times, the speaker will be talking about a subject that the audience is familiar with but there are also times when a speaker may be talking about a subject that not all audience members are experts in. The speaker needs to help the audience get to a certain 'base' of understanding (not assuming anything about what the audience knows or does not know) and then expand that understanding as the speech progresses.

2. Laying out the structure of the speech / what the speaker will talk about - The best outcome for any speech is for the audience to take action because of what they learned during the speech. If the audience does not understand the speech, they will certainly not know what action to take, much less take any action at all. The best way for the audience to understand the speech is to provide them with a structure and outline of how the speech will be laid out so that the audience can easily follow along.

3. Hinting or identifying what the conclusion of the speech will be (i.e., what will the audience takeaway after the speech) - Again, this is linked to the audience's understanding of your speech - what will the audience get out of this speech and what should they be looking for? For example, if your speech's key takeaway is that meditation is good for you, the audience will be looking for both logical and emotional arguments to either persuade them or if they already knew, what else could convince them to give it more focus.

Consider these objectives as you are evaluating the speech introduction.

Things to look for:

* Does the speaker say thank you

The speaker does not need to say thank you at all. The audience should be thanking the speaker for taking the time to prepare and deliver the speech.

*** Does the speaker apologize for lack of preparation **

The speaker should not be apologizing for a lack of preparation; the biggest reason for this is that the audience has no idea and only by apologizing does the audience truly know that the speaker did not prepare. It also does not give a strong impression to the audience because the audience is giving their time to listen to the speaker and in exchange for their valuable time, the speaker delivers something that is lackluster.

* Does the speaker acknowledge the audience

I believe that a speaker cannot effectively engage the audience without first acknowledging that they are speaking to them. If you go onto youtube and check out any speeches delivered in a formal setting (e.g., Conan O'Brien White House Correspondent's Dinner), you will see that the speaker addresses everyone (and usually the most important people first). For that matter, it is also important for the speaker to acknowledge the host or whoever introduces them to speak. For instance, let's say the President of the United States is in attendance at a meeting. Bill introduces you. The speaker's first words are generally along the lines of "Thank you Bill. Mr. President of the United States" and then they would continue acknowledging other members of the audience.

I also see a lot of speakers going into their speech right away and acknowledging the audience later - this is perfectly fine, as long as they are acknowledging the audience in some way.

* Does the speech introduction start off strongly?

Does it engage the audience right away? - In my opinion, there are three ways to start off strongly in a speech: a rhetorical question, a surprising fact or statement, and a quote. That is not to say that if a speaker does not start in one of these three ways, it will not be a strong introduction but if a speech's introduction is weak, it might be because they did not start in one of these three ways.

A speech's introduction should draw the audience into the speech and as an evaluator, you can see if this was done effectively by watching how the audience is reacting to the speech introduction. Are they leaning in? Are they paying attention? Are they nodding their heads or laughing along with the speech?

I also see a lot of speakers asking questions (and not just rhetorical questions) to the audience and this can be an effective way of engaging the audience if done effectively. What makes an effective question? The evaluator should look for how the question ties into the overall flow of the speech introduction. "How many of you look at your phones in bed?" *Several hands are raised* "Did you know that this can drastically affect the quantity and quality of your sleep?"

* Do you (and the audience) understand what the purpose of the speech is - Every speech has both a general purpose and a specific purpose. Although the introduction of the speaker should have this information, the speaker may also talk about their purpose indirectly. They may not explicitly say that they are trying to inform the audience but if the subject or speech title is "How to think like an entrepreneur" then the audience knows implicitly that the speaker is teaching them something. This purpose can be tremendously important to an evaluator because ultimately, at the end of the speech, the evaluator (that's you) has to decide whether or not the speaker achieved their purpose and how effective they were in achieving that purpose.

* Does the speaker introduce the speech topic / subject with sufficient background and context

This depends on the speech subject and the audience. A doctor talking to an audience full of doctors and health practitioners about the latest cancer treatments probably does not need to go over what cancer is but, if relevant to the talk / treatment, perhaps the doctor will need to talk about the mechanisms through which cancer spreads. Whenever I hear a speech, I think about how educated the audience needs to be in order to understand the speech. Conversely, some of the best speeches are universal and easy to understand by any audience. How does an evaluator know that a speech introduction has provided sufficient background and context? In my opinion, I won't know until I have heard the whole speech because I do not necessarily know what will be covered until after I hear the whole speech. Once I have finished hearing the speech, I think back to the introduction and the body to see if there were any gaps in the flow of the overall speech. Was there some background information that was implied or assumed in order for the speech to work? Was the speaker careful in providing enough background and context for the audience? Did the speaker look for audience cues that told him / her that the audience was getting lost? These are all good things to look for as an evaluator in order to understand whether the introduction provided enough context for the overall speech.

* Does the speaker lay out what he / she will be talking about in the speech

Once the speaker has provided enough background for their speech, I believe they should be then laying out exactly what they will be talking about in their speech. This of course, depends on the speech content but after the speech introduction, an audience generally has a good understanding of what the speaker's purpose will be and what they will be taking away after the speech. A good speech introduction will often provide a brief outline of the overall speech before proceeding into the speech body and this will help the audience follow along as the speech progresses.

Body - what to look for

A speech body has three objectives that an evaluator should be considering:

1. The speech body should try to build on the speech introduction. The speech introduction may allude to the key takeaway that the audience will get and therefore, the speech body will describe the main arguments and points that build and lead to that key takeaway.

2. The speech body should try to follow the structure as outlined by the speech introduction - If the speaker has provided a structure or outline of their speech in their introduction, the speech body should follow that outline to make it easy for the audience to follow.

If the speech introduction did not talk about the structure of their speech, how easy is it for the audience to follow the speech body? Are there framing statements (e.g., I just finished talking about X and now I'm going to talk about Y) that help the audience understand the overall speech?

3. The speech body should create the foundation for an effective conclusion - the speech body will lead to a specific conclusion or takeaway for the audience. Did it miss anything? Are there arguments or points that the speaker did not cover in their speech that should have been covered? Think about your own experience and what parts of the speech you may have been confused about - did the speech address those points?

Here are some things to watch for in the speech body:

* If appropriate, examine the arguments that the speaker provides

Is the speaker trying to persuade you of something? Are the arguments laid out so that it is easy to follow and the audience can logically build on each argument to get to the conclusion? Are there any arguments missing?

* Are there supporting facts, statements, anecdotes, etc. to support the speech

It is not just about providing supporting facts or statistics but it is also about providing relevant statements that add to the speech's purpose and build on the speech introduction. If the speaker is discussing ways to save money, is the speaker sharing tips that everyone can use or only people with a certain skill set or profession can use?

Are the tips realistic? How much money can you save compared to the effort that you need? Does the speaker have personal experience? Has the speaker used the tips themselves to save money? In this example, these are all things for the speech evaluator to consider when trying to evaluate how effective a speech body is given the purpose. A similar evaluation following a similar but adapted framework will need to be done for different speeches.

* Are there enough 'paragraphs' for the speech

Although not a strict rule, I try to aim for three paragraphs or three different arguments in my speech body. If my speech is on ways to become a better speaker, I might focus on three specific things that I think would help speakers the most (speech organization, body language, strong introduction and conclusion).

As a speech evaluator, I try to figure out how many paragraphs a speaker has in his speech and then understand, at the end, whether this was enough to support the speech purpose. It is of course different for different speeches (e.g., a speech that is a single story will not have this) but as a way of understanding things, people generally try to break things down into bigger chunks and that's why I look for paragraphs as an evaluator.

* Are there appropriate transitions between 'paragraphs'

There may be a lot of supporting facts, statements, anecdotes or statistics but how are they formed into paragraphs? And how are they joined from one paragraph to another? Look for connecting words such as "however, therefore, consequently, subsequently, first, second, third, etc."

These are all words that help the audience understand how different clauses are connected and which clauses are important. These words also help to build the story in the audience's mind on exactly the takeaway that the speaker is sharing with the audience.

Conclusion - what to look for

A conclusion also, in my opinion, has three objectives:

1. To summarize the major points that have been shared in the speech - If the speaker has shared a lot of points in their speech, it can be difficult for the audience to remember everything. The speaker should make it as easy as possible to help the audience understand everything about their speech and their key takeaway.

2. To share the next steps, if applicable - It is good for the speaker to assume that their speech has persuaded the audience to take action. Outlining the next steps for the audience can help the audience understand where they can find more information or how easy the next steps are if they wanted to take action. Although it is likely that not all audience members will be persuaded, some will and they will no doubt be looking for how they can take the next step.

3. To provide a takeaway to the audience / convince the audience to take action - What does the speaker want the audience to understand at the end of their speech? Was the speaker successful in providing that key takeaway to the audience with supporting facts or arguments? As an evaluator, one of your responsibilities is to understand what you took away from the speech and whether you were convinced.

Here are some things to watch for in the speech conclusion:

* Did the speaker thank the audience at the end?

There is no need for the speaker to thank the audience after the speech and I think that in place of "thank you", there are stronger ways to end speeches. The audience should be thanking the speaker for preparing and delivering the speech.

* Did the speaker end strongly?

Did the speech conclusion leave you feeling energized and motivated? Or did it leave you feeling confused and bored? How did you feel at the end of the speech? With great speeches, the audience will understand and internalize the key takeaway of the speech and leave the speech feeling excited to take the next steps.

* Did the speaker build on the speech body?

One way to build on the speech body is to save your best argument or point for last (i.e., the conclusion). This can be a great way to slowly persuade or convince the audience on your main purpose and then to really solidify that argument with your best point. Rather than just re-iterating the points made in the speech in different words, did the speaker try to share a conclusion that builds on those points?

* How did the audience react?

Did you notice a change in their body language from the start of their speech to the end? Do they seem more receptive to the speaker? Are they attentive? Are they nodding their heads and do they agree with what the speaker is talking about? This can be a great way to gauge how effective the audience has been (in addition to understanding how you felt about the speech).

* How did the speaker end?

Speeches can end in many different ways so observe how the speaker ended their speech. Did they end with a relevant quote? Did they create a call to action? A speaker chooses how they end their speech but in your opinion, was it the best way to end their speech or could they have concluded in a more effective manner?

Chapter 4 – After the speech (providing an oral evaluation)

Evaluation structures

You have finished hearing the speech, all the while taking notes on the strengths and the opportunities for improvement for the speaker. Hopefully your notes are organized in some way (I provided a way to organize the notes in an earlier chapter) and now is the time to provide an oral evaluation to the speaker.

The first thing to do is to figure out how you want to structure your oral evaluation. In Toastmasters, one of the techniques that is taught is using something called the 'sandwich' technique. It is called the sandwich technique because it sandwiches constructive criticism with positive feedback. For example, "Joe, you show great confidence in your speech by coming close to the audience and maintaining strong eye contact. I did think that you moved too much though and in my opinion, it is better to move to one side of the room, speak for at least a paragraph before moving again but I thought you used the whole stage well".

There are a variety of structures that you can use for speech evaluations and I provide a few of these below:

* 3 - 2 - 1: In this speech evaluation, the speech evaluator provides three positive comments about the speech / speaker, two comments about the opportunities for improvement and finally one positive comment where the speech evaluator thought that the speech / speaker was most effective (or it can also be your favourite thing about the speech).

1. Positive points (something the speaker did well) x3
2. Constructive criticisms (an opportunity for improvement for the speaker) x2
3. Your favourite thing about the speech / the speech's best attribute

* **Modified sandwich technique**: There are a few gaps that other Toastmasters have found with the normal sandwich technique. For instance the fact that people remember the first and last thing in the evaluation means that if the opportunities for improvement are in the middle of the evaluation, the speaker may not remember everything. The modified sandwich technique is similar to the sandwich technique: it starts off with positive comments about the speaker's abilities, areas for the speaker to improve but it ends with specific examples and suggestions for improving the speech.

1. Positive points (something the speaker did well) x3

2. Constructive criticisms (an opportunity for improvement for the speaker) x3
3. Specific examples and suggestions for improving the speech x3

* **3 - 3 - recap:** Another technique that I've seen a speaker use in an award winning evaluation is the 3 - 3 - recap (the name of the structure I just came up with because I wasn't sure if there was a name for the technique). It involves providing three very specific positive comments about what the speaker did well in their speech, three specific suggestions for improvement (with examples pulled from the speech and suggestions for improving on those areas) and finally, a short recap or summary of the evaluation with a call to action at the end.

1. Positive points (something the speaker did well) x3
2. Constructive criticisms (an opportunity for improvement for the speaker) x3
3. Recap of the positive points and areas for improvement

* **Sandwich technique:**
Here is a structure that I like to use for my speech evaluations. It is called the 'sandwich' technique because it sandwiches constructive criticism with positive comments about the speech.

1. General comments about how you felt about the speech
2. Positive points (something the speaker did well) x3
3. Constructive criticisms (an opportunity for improvement for the speaker) x3

4. The speaker's best strength (or what you liked best about the speech)
5. Final comments congratulating the speaker and looking forward to their next speech

Tips on providing an oral evaluation

Here are some general tips that I think would help you, as an evaluator, give a good speech evaluation:

* Greet the audience and thank the speaker at the start

As an evaluator, you, in a way, represent the audience's thoughts and thanking the speaker can be an effective way of putting the speaker in a good mood and reminding them that you are not there to bring the speaker down from a great speech but to help him / her improve for future speeches.

* Follow a structure / framework for your speech

Just like a regular speech, a speech evaluation should have a structure for the audience to follow. Perhaps in between 4 and 5 above, I might say "I'd like to suggest three opportunities for improvement for your next speech. One, X.... Two, Y.... Three, Z..." In this way, it is easy for the audience to follow and easy for you to summarize the opportunities for improvement in your speech conclusion as well.

* End on a positive note

Although you may have identified various opportunities for improvement for the speaker, the speaker has taken the time to create and deliver this speech and as an evaluator, you should be congratulating them on their speech and motivating them to deliver more (and better) speeches in the future. Ending on a positive note helps to also ease the 'pain' of hearing constructive criticism for the speaker.

* If you think there are a lot of opportunities for improvement, choose three areas for your speech evaluation

Try to balance your speech evaluation towards the positive notes. If your whole speech evaluation is on opportunities for improvement, it makes it seem like the evaluator (you) is showing the audience how bad the speech was and the speaker may not be motivated to give another speech in the future. Choose three points for improvement and leave the rest to be shared privately with the speaker after. Which three should you choose? Try to choose points for improvement that will help the speaker the most if they addressed these in their next speech.

* Try to provide specific examples of what the speaker did and how the speaker can improve

Examples are the best way to clarify exactly what the speaker did in their speech and how they can improve. "During your presentation, I noticed that you turned your back to the audience. It is much better to be facing the audience because not only will your voice be projecting towards the audience but you will also be maintaining good eye contact and engaging the audience better when you are facing them."

* Use personal statements as much as possible

I believe, in my opinion, etc. Wide sweeping statements like "You should have" or "It's apparent that" make it seem like there is a right and a wrong way of speaking and that is not the case at all. The points that you have jotted down and shared are based on your personal opinion and how you perceived the speech and not based on anyone else's perception.

Chapter 5

Sample evaluations

The following sample evaluations have been provided to help you understand the notes that I take when I evaluate speakers as well as the way I structure my evaluation speech when providing an oral evaluation to speakers. Although I did not record or write down my exact speeches word for word, I will provide a sample evaluation speech so that you can see how I build the evaluations from my notes.

As mentioned previously, I like to break down my notes into three sections: Introduction, Body and Conclusion. Under each section, and as I hear the speaker speak, I write down quick notes on what I thought was strong and what I thought could be improved. Each note has either a "+" or a "-" depending on whether it is a strength or whether it is an opportunity for improvement. If you divide the paper into three columns, I draw a line for the last third of the page and use that section as a way to structure my oral evaluation (i.e., the first 2 columns of the page are for my notes for when I'm listening to the speech and the last column of the page are for my notes when I am doing the evaluation speech).

Sample evaluation #1

In this speech, the speaker was working on their Icebreaker project (the first speech out of the Toastmasters Competent Communication manual). The speaker is a brand new Toastmaster having only joined the club for a month.

My notes

Intro:

- good hand gestures
    - hands on the hip, hands in pockets

Body:

- eye contact is fleeting, down to the ground
- "like" - informal language

Conclusion:

+ ended strongly

My speaking notes

+ memorized your speech
+ good flow
+ good hand gestures (at times, your hands were on your hips or in your pockets)

- eye contact (looked around the room but it was sometimes down to the ground)
- informal language

+ ended strongly and it left us wanting more

Sample evaluation speech based on my speaking notes

Thank you "X", your speech was very good and you obviously have great speaking abilities. I saw a lot of your strengths come out of the speech.

You had great preparation - you memorized your speech and you came out in front of the lectern to speak to the audience which also shows you had confidence in yourself. It's not a common thing that I see with icebreakers and I commend you on your confidence to come closer to the audience and engage them more effectively than if you were behind the lectern. The overall flow and structure of your speech was also quite good - I could easily follow along and that helped me and the audience to understand what you were going to say and where you were headed.

In terms of opportunities for improvement, I challenge you to improve two things for your future speech. First, although your eye contact was good around the room, it was too quick to make a connection with the audience member. In addition, there were times where you were thinking about the next thing to say and your eye contact went down to the ground. Try to hold your eye contact for at least a sentence or two and then move on to the next audience member and although it is difficult, try to stare straight ahead while thinking of the next thing to say. This will require practice but it will also help you maintain that crucial connection with the audience.

My second challenge for you is to try to eliminate some of your informal language. I heard "like" and "you know" and your speech can be much stronger if you eliminate these words, which may even become crutch words if you use them too frequently.

Overall, I believe that you possess many great speaking skills including creating a strong structure for your speech and showing confidence by coming in front of the lectern. For next time, you can work on maintaining your eye contact with the audience and removing informal language. My favourite part about your speech was how strong the conclusion was and how it left the audience wanting to hear more. Thank you for your speech and I look forward to hearing your next speech.

Sample evaluation #2

In this speech, the speaker was working on a project with visual aids (the projector). He was discussing the different projects he has worked on as part of his career. As a side note, the speaker has his Distinguished Toastmaster designation and has done over 50 speeches; understanding the speaker's current level can help to focus your evaluation on things of value (e.g., they probably do not need any feedback on speech organization).

My notes

Intro:

- providing the background / context for the speech may be more appropriate as part of the speaker introduction

Body:

+ very good way of engaging the audience
+ stories were relevant
        + showed breadth and depth of experience you have
+ good structure (problem statement, vision, solution, lessons learned)
+ good hand gestures
+ simple explanations with easy to understand language

Conclusion:

+ ended strongly by recapping the projects and the lessons you have learned

My speaking notes

+ projects were fascinating
+ good hand gestures
+ simple explanations with no jargon

- enhance your speaker introduction to include the background / context for your speech
- limit the number of projects that you talk about in order to cut down on your speech time

+ great personal anecdotes that enhanced the projects
+ you have great breadth and depth of experience

Sample evaluation speech based on my speaking notes

Thank you "X", you wowed me with the projects that you have worked on and your passion and enthusiasm for your career is really infectious - I wish I was able to work on similar projects in my career. I thought that the structure that you used was quite effective with a problem statement, vision, solution and lessons learned - this structure really helped me understand the project that you worked on as well as the lessons that others might be able to take away from that project.

You had good visual aids but I also thought your hand gestures helped to add to the various projects and anecdotes you shared with us. Another thing I thought you did well was how simple and easy to understand the explanations were - I did not detect any jargon at all. I thought there were two ways that your speech could have been better and I encourage you to look at these two areas for future speeches: one, you used a bit of time at the beginning to explain your speech and your career and I thought you could have done this in the speaker's introduction rather than in your actual speech - this would help you to cut down on your speech time as I think you went over your time limit. The other thing that I think would help to stay within the time limit is to limit the number of projects that you talked about. I think all of them were fascinating but cutting down to two or three projects would help you better stay within the time limit. My favourite thing about your speech were the short anecdotes that you shared in addition to the projects themselves - they really helped to give life to the projects and shows the breadth and depth of your experience. Thank you for sharing all of these great projects you've worked on.

Sample evaluation #3

This speaker was working on Project 2 from the Competent Communication manual (Organize your speech). This Toastmaster is not a new Toastmaster but they have not been doing speeches and so they have only started their 2nd speech even after being a member for 6 months.

My notes

Intro:

+ rhetorical question to engage the audience

Body:

+ good hand gestures
+ good use of the speaking space
+ three principles
>   + think long term
>   + live simply
>   + maximize value

- informal language "you know", "okay"

Conclusion:

+ recap of three points

My speaking notes

+ great engagement of the audience through rhetorical questions, real life examples and interacting with the audience
+ good structure that is easy to follow
+ good hand gestures and good use of the speaking space

- some colloquial language that could be removed to make the speech more polished
- the paragraphs did not seem balanced (there was more content in the first and third principle)

+ timely and relevant content
+ practical examples derived from living and breathing the three principles

Sample evaluation speech based on my speaking notes
Thank you "X", I enjoyed this speech because I know how frugal you are. One of the objectives of your speech was to organize your speech in such a way that it enhances the message and content of your speech and I thought that the structure of your speech was well laid out. You organized your speech around three principles and in addition to explaining each principle, you also provided us with great examples on how to follow these principles in real life. You also have good hand gestures and good use of the speaking space.

I thought there were two things that you can work on for next time. One, you had some informal language that I thought took away from the speech. Minimizing the informal language will really help to polish your speech. Two, I personally felt that the three paragraphs were not balanced. There seemed to be more speaking and content in the first and third paragraph so adding a sentence or two to the second principle would have helped to balance it out for me.

Overall, you had good structure and hand gestures. In order to polish your speech, minimize the informal language that you had and try to balance the content as much as possible between the three principles. What I liked the most about your speech was the fact that you had great examples for each principle - it shows us that you really have lived and breathed these principles and you know what you are talking about.

Sample evaluation #4

This speaker is a brand new Toastmaster who was working on their icebreaker (the very first speech out of the Competent Communication manual). Generally for icebreakers, the evaluator will focus more on encouraging the speaker rather than the critique. The icebreaker is a chance for the speaker to discover the speaking skills they already have and therefore, your role as an evaluator is to point out those skills and to point their attention to the skills that may need to be refined (while keeping in mind that they have many more projects to work through to improve some of those skills like organizing the speech and vocal variety).

My notes

Intro:

Body:
+ good eye contact
+ good volume
+ good concentration / focus
+ good humour
+ showed confidence
+ hand gestures made the speech more effective

- a few crutch words and informal language: "now", "you know", "right"
- lacked a speech outline / structure

Conclusion:

My speaking notes

+ good eye contact
+ volume was great
+ good humour
+ showed a lot of confidence

- crutch words
- a speech structure will help make the speech more effective
- conclusion can have a key takeaway for the audience

Sample evaluation speech based on my speaking notes

Thank you "X" for your icebreaker. I always enjoy icebreakers because it is a fantastic opportunity for all members to learn more about new members. You already possess a lot of great speaking skills: your eye contact is good, the volume of your voice is strong and can be heard by everyone, there was a few distractions here and there but you had great concentration in maintaining your speech. You also show a lot of confidence by engaging with the audience and using humour.

I thought there are two things that you can look at improving for next time: one, you had some informal language within your speech. For example, I heard "now", "you know" and "right" and I think if this can be minimized, your speech would be much more effective. Two, although this will be something that you will work on in Project 2, I thought that your speech could use a bit more structure so that it is easier for the audience to follow. I use a technique called "signposting" in order to help me structure my speech. I tell the audience what I am going to say, I tell the audience and then I tell the audience what I just told them. It is a simple but effective way in helping the audience understand what I discussed in my speech.

Again, in summary, you possess a lot of great speaking skills, which makes me think that this isn't your first time getting up to speak. Minimizing your crutch words and framing your speech with more structure will help make your next speech more effective. Thank you for sharing your personal stories and for sharing something about yourself. I look forward to your next speech.

www.ingramcontent.com/pod-product-compliance
Lightning Source LLC
Chambersburg PA
CBHW071012180526
45168CB00003B/1388